Setting the scene ...

An ace reporter always writes the best stories. Brendan Sloan is waiting for the delivery of a new video game. Then he will be able to write a *really* good story for the neighborhood newspaper. But while he waits, some very strange things happen.

What *will* Brendan Sloan write about?

very exciting could happen ..."

Chapter 1.

Meet Brendan Sloan, ace reporter for *The South Street News*. Brendan sat on his bike, pretending to read a comic. He was really working on another big story. He waited and watched as shoppers rushed around Main Street. Soon, something very exciting should happen!

Ace Reporter

Written by Quentin Flynn

Illustrated by Lloyd Foye

Contents	Page
Chapter 1. *A big story*	4
Chapter 2. *An odd thing*	9
Chapter 3. *Brendan keeps watch*	15
Chapter 4. *More strange events*	18
Chapter 5. *A brainstorm!*	26
Verse	32

Ace Reporter

With these characters ...

Brendan Sloan

Miss Miller

Mr. Fizzlewell

Mrs. Borderline

Mr. Curdle

"Any moment now, something

   Brendan had heard that the toy store was getting a delivery of the latest video game from Japan. As soon as it was delivered, he would rush in and buy the first copy of "Robo-Rabbit Racer"!

Wow! He would be the first kid to play Robo-Rabbit Racer. He would also be the first reporter to write about it for *The South Street News*. Then Brendan would still be an ace reporter. He would also be the coolest kid in the neighborhood!

Brendan looked at his watch. Ten minutes to nine. He checked his camera. When the delivery truck arrived, Brendan would be ready to take the first photo.

Chapter 2.

Brendan was daydreaming about racing Robo-Rabbits when a van appeared. But it wasn't a toy delivery truck. Brendan saw the lady from the health food store driving the van. Miss Miller drove her van up to Roly-Poly's Burgers next to the toy store.

"That's odd," thought Brendan. "Miss Miller is always telling me not to eat too much fast food. I'll hide close by to hear what she orders."

Miss Miller spoke into the speaker. "Hi, Penny. I want to order the usual please."

Then Brendan heard Penny's reply from the speaker.

"Five Roly-Poly burgers with deep-fried cheese lumps, six cartons of deep-fried french fries, two ice-cream sundaes with caramel topping, and a Roly-Poly fudge pie? Is that all?"

"Yes, thanks! The same as yesterday," nodded Miss Miller, licking her lips. "Here's twenty dollars. Keep the change."

Penny staggered out to Miss Miller's van, carrying all of the food.
Miss Miller couldn't wait to put a handful of french fries in her mouth.

"See you tomorrow," said Miss Miller. She drove off with her mouth full.

"That's strange," thought Brendan. "Oh well, I'd better go back and watch the toy store. The delivery truck should be here soon."

Brendan looked at his watch again. He took a photo of his shoe, just to make sure his camera was working. He heard an engine coming closer. Was this the delivery truck? Brendan got ready to run.

Chapter 3.

Brendan was upset. The engine sound didn't come from the delivery truck. Instead, Brendan saw a pink sports car speeding up the street. It sped through a yellow light. Brendan could hear the thump-thump-thump of loud music coming from inside the car.

"That driver must think this is a Robo-Rabbit racetrack," thought Brendan.

Suddenly, a police car drove in behind the sports car with a red light flashing. The sports car screeched to a stop. Then Mr. Fizzlewell, the banker, climbed out. He was chewing bubblegum. He wore purple jeans and a bright green shirt.

"Wow!" thought Brendan. "He sure looks different when he's not at the bank."

Brendan watched as a policewoman got out of the police car. She started to write out a speeding ticket.

"This is your fourth speeding ticket this week, sir," she said.

The policewoman gave Mr. Fizzlewell the speeding ticket. Mr. Fizzlewell waited until she drove away. Then he sped off again.

Brendan couldn't believe what he saw! He started to watch the toy store again. The Robo-Rabbit Racer was more important than Mr. Fizzlewell. He crossed his fingers and hoped it would be delivered soon. Now he was hungry. He only had a squashy banana in his bag. "I'm not *that* hungry yet," he thought.

Chapter 4.

Brendan looked at his watch again. Only ten minutes had gone by since he last checked his watch. He was bored.

Out of the corner of his eye, he saw Mrs. Borderline, the librarian. She was walking her dalmatian in the park.

Just then, she unleashed her dog. The dog ran to a flower bed and dug up some flowers. The dog ran back and Mrs. Borderline put the leash back on the dog. Then she quickly walked away, without replanting the flowers.

Brendan walked over to take a photo of the dug-up flowers. Just then his friend, Jim, stopped on his skateboard. He asked Brendan if he wanted to play softball.

Brendan *really* wanted to play softball. He was still bored. But the toy delivery truck might arrive at any moment. After all this time waiting, he would hate to miss it!

Three hours later, there was still no delivery truck. Brendan had even eaten the squashy banana. He wondered what else he could write about for the front page of *The South Street News*.

Just as he was about to leave, someone parked their car in front of a "No Parking" sign. Mr. Curdle, the hobby store owner, got out and stuck a note to his windshield. He strolled into the Jubilee Jelly Beans store.

Brendan walked closer and squinted his eyes. He could just read the note.

"Emergency: Doctor on Duty," it said.

"That's strange," thought Brendan. "I didn't know Mr. Curdle was a doctor, too."

A police officer came along to write out a parking ticket. After he read the note on Mr. Curdle's car windshield, he walked away. Then Mr. Curdle came out with a huge bag of jelly beans. He giggled when he saw that the police officer hadn't written him a ticket.

Brendan was shocked! But all he could think about was his story for the newspaper. It was now five o'clock. Robo-Rabbit Racer wasn't going to be delivered today. This was a disaster! Brendan Sloan, ace reporter for *The South Street News*, didn't have anything to write about.

Chapter 5.

As Brendan rode home, he thought he might see more people out doing strange things.

He called the editor of *The South Street News*.

"What happened?" asked Kylie excitedly.

"Nothing," replied Brendan glumly. "The toy delivery truck didn't show up. I waited all day and *nothing* happened."

"Oh, no!" said Kylie. "That means there's no news for the front page of next week's newspaper!"

"Don't worry about it. I'll think of something," said Brendan. He hung up the phone. Then he stared at the blank computer screen.

Suddenly, he had a brainstorm! He smiled a sneaky-looking smile. Why hadn't he thought of this before? He would make a crossword puzzle! And it would be even better than a Robo-Rabbit Racer story!

Brendan typed in the clues as fast as his fingers could move. When he had finished the crossword puzzle, he printed it out. As he proofread the clues, he knew that he was still an ace reporter.

All the kids in the neighborhood — *and* the adults — would be racing each other to figure out the answers!

An Ace Crossword

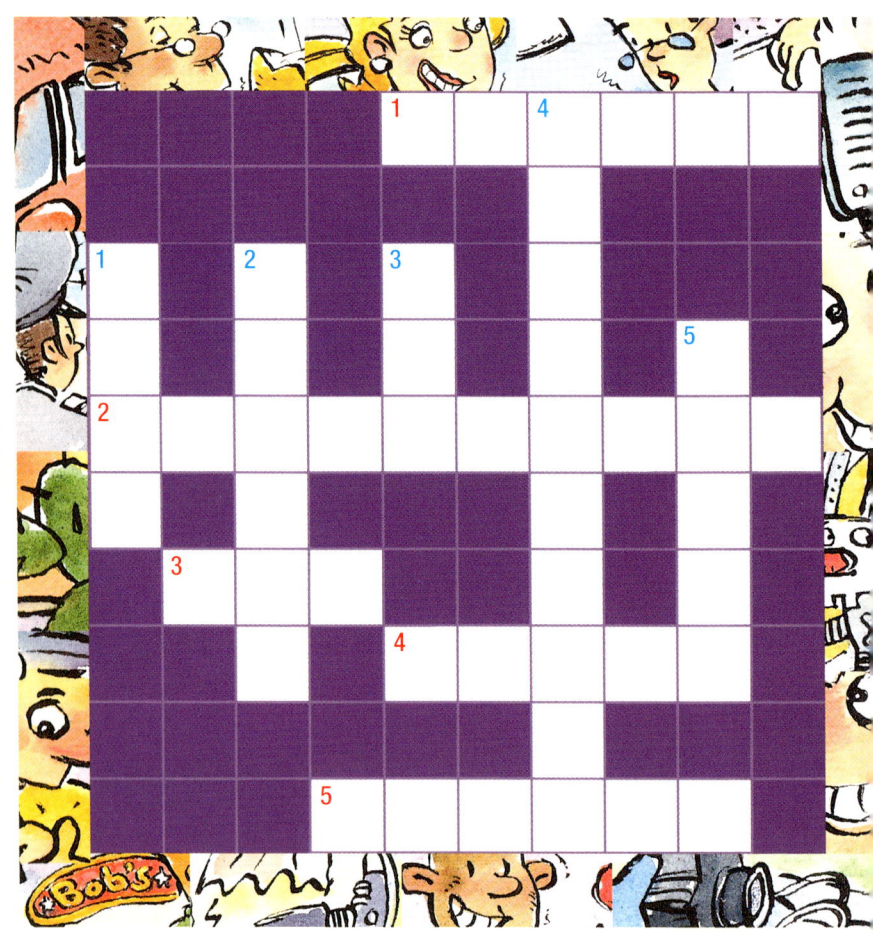

Across

1. When someone parks where they shouldn't, it is _ _ _ _ _ _ to other drivers.

2. Mrs. _ _ _ _ _ _ _ _ _ _ _'_ dog dug up flowers in the flower bed.

3. Eating Roly-Poly burgers for breakfast could make you feel _ _ _.

4. If your dog makes a mess, you should _ _ _ _ _ it up.

5. Miss _ _ _ _ _ _ should eat more healthy foods.

Down

1. A kind of Rabbit Racer.

2. Mr. _ _ _ _ _ _ should not pretend to be a doctor.

3. Brendan Sloan is an _ _ _ reporter.

4. Mr. _ _ _ _ _ _ _ _ _ should drive a lot more carefully.

5. A person driving a pink sports car should drive _ _ _ _ _ the speed limit.

"On The Trail"

AN A**C**E REPORTER

IS ON THE T**R**AIL

OF A ST**O**RY

THAT'S INTERE**S**TING

AND **S**O COOL!

THESE **W**ORDS WILL TEL

WHAT OUR REP**O**RTER SAW

WHEN EACH PE**R**SON

IGNORE**D** A RULE!